What others are saying about
Una Lisa Williams . . .

"I have personally watched and admired Lisa's accomplishments both from up close and afar. It does not matter what setting she is in, be it work, church, or home, her humble demeanor is constant and uplifting. No matter the role in which she serves or the task she is given, she accepts it and commits to it with a passion. This book, along with her personal insights as a parent, spiritual leader, and civil servant, beautifully demonstrates her character as a "servant leader.""

-Kathy Monroe, L CIV USARMY 106 SIG BDE

"I had the privilege to serve in the US Army with Una Lisa Williams for four years. She is a very professional non-commissioned officer who always accomplished the mission set before her, and who placed the welfare of her soldiers above her own. She was respected by them and admired by the leadership, so it is no surprise that Ms. Williams was named the 2017 Oklahoma Woman Veteran of the year. She continues to serve the community and veteran organizations, and she is active in her church. Now as an author, she has focused her passion and directed her work to help teenagers and young adults. Rarely do we see people with so much personnel drive and commitment to serve others. If you are in a room with Ms. Williams, you quickly realize there is something special about her. I have truly been honored to know her. I am certain you will be highly inspired with her book."

-Marty Talley, CSM (R) USARMY

"I am honored to have had the opportunity to read, study, and meditate on the words in this book. I am so proud of Una Lisa. She and I grew up together in the same city and attended the same schools through high school. I also followed in her footsteps and joined the US Army. We were stationed on the same installation where we "found" each other and we have not lost contact since. The importance of her introducing this book at this profound time is significant; it is a teaching tool for our millennials. The short prayers will resonate with both younger and older generations. This book is not merely for teenagers or young adults, but for anyone who can envision fostering a better life. It will encourage you to navigate through life empowered. It will help you gain confidence, embrace life's challenges with a positive outlook, adopt healthier choices, improve your mindset, and focus on doing what's right regardless of who is watching. These are quality attributes that can and will lead to a blessed and productive life. Moreover, to know that your voice matters, your life matters, there is hope in spite of your circumstances, and that you are chosen and

not a mistake is enough to motivate you to embrace the pursuit of your dreams. Wow, this book is powerful and invaluable! Read it, meditate on it, and put these awesome tools to great use and you are sure to keep swimming. This book can impact a small reading group, a school, or a community if even a few of these principles are applied.
Trust and believe."

-Angelina R. Broom-Brooks, Mckinney, TX

"I met Una Lisa over 20 years ago while we were both stationed in the same unit in Oklahoma. She was a very direct, well organized, hard-charging soldier. My first impression of her was that either we were going to bump heads or we would become friends. It turned out better than that: we developed a true brother and sister relationship. Una Lisa has been a single mother who has worked tirelessly to provide the best for her son, while being a professional in whatever she does. One of the great things about Una Lisa is that she never, ever, accepts anything being half way done; it must be done right, the first time! She pours her heart and soul into giving to others. She has not only provided for her son, but through her generosity and unselfish living, she has provided food, clothing, shelter, and a strong shoulder to lean on to many others. She is truly a God-fearing woman who loves the Lord and this book is the result of her obedience to His will. This work comes from a heart that's larger than Texas. I honestly believe it will touch hearts, open eyes, and save many lives. This is a positive book written to encourage and motivate those who may feel they have no hope. Your environment and circumstances cannot inhibit your desire to be successful. Our young people today need to know they can achieve their heart's desires and can be whatever or whomever they choose. *Predestined to Soar: Rise to See Who You Were Meant to Be* is an uplifting book for the soul. Once you read this book, you will realize how truly blessed you are."

-Michael Chatman Sr., M.Ed., Georgetown, TX

"Without a doubt, the most powerful concept this book introduces us to is *unconditional love by the Creator*. I believe that He is watching over us and regardless of our present situation, there is always a "safe space" to have a happy and healthy life. The interpretation of happy and healthy can be different based on personality or the current state people are in, however, as is expressed in these pages, the love He has for you will always bring you to peace and provide you with comfort. Una Lisa Williams is a strong believer in making a difference in her community. I was able to experience it myself. Her faith in God—and her passion to reach out to others and share God's words with them—has motivated her to take action and write this book to show the power of God's love. While working with her, I learned to be positive and keep my dreams in perspective, regardless of the obstacles that may be on my way. Her determination to see people succeed and transformed by the power of God's love has really guided her work and impacted people all around her. What a blessing to have worked with her! This book is exceptional in every way. William's dedication and her ability to strengthen others by the power of God shine through on every page."

-*Iwona Jeanbaptiste, Wiesbaden, Germany*

Who do you turn to when the encourager needs encouraging? Where do you go when the motivator needs motivating? And who do you call when you want to make sense of the nonsense going on in the local community? First of all, you call on God. Then, you call on my sister, friend, and confidant "Lisa." Her busy schedule does not detract her from making time for friends or strangers in need of an uplifting word or an act of kindness. "True in word and deed" is her motto, and she lives up to her commitment to make this world a better place. I know from personal experience that *unconditional love* is not a cliché. If you are loved by Lisa, you are guaranteed that it's unconditional. *Predestined to Soar* is a thought-provoking, action-driven book from the vantage point of someone who overcame many barriers and obstacles in her life, and used the lessons learned—and her relationship with God—to inspire others to overcome. It is a how-to manual to get you on track using biblical principles to guide you through the challenges of life. Written especially for teenagers and young adults, I found the information and guidance a reminder to stimulate, re-energize, and refocus on some goals, visions, and dreams I have yet to fulfill. Designed as a self-help book, it graciously points us to our "Present Help" while uncovering the weaknesses and challenges we face. At the same time it helps us strengthen those areas where we are strong. It provokes us to look inside ourselves, evaluate the things before us, and make the changes that propel us to become who we were meant to be.

-First Lady Avril Adams-Williams,
Triumphant Church International Ministries

Predestined to Soar

PREDESTINED TO SOAR

Predestined to Soar

RISE TO SEE WHO YOU WERE MEANT TO BE

Una Lisa Williams

Splendor Publishing
College Station, TX

Predestined to Soar: Rise to See Who You Were Meant to Be

First published printing, May, 2018.

SPLENDOR PUBLISHING
Published by Splendor Publishing
College Station, TX.

Library of Congress Control Number: 2017962282
Predestined to Soar: Rise to See Who You Were Meant to Be

ISBN-10: 1-940278-23-6
ISBN-13: 978-1-940278-23-0
1. Self-help 2. Spirituality

Printed in the United States of America.

Cover Photo: © Paul Moore | Dreamstime.com

Back Cover Photo (Una Lisa Williams):
Photographer, Kirstyn Reyes with *Captured by Kiki.*

For more information or to order bulk copies of this book for events,
seminars, conferences, youth assemblies, or training, please contact
us at SplendorPublishing.com.

Dedication

This book is dedicated to all teenagers and young adults around the world. This book is especially dedicated to my son, who stated to me over twenty years ago, "Mom, you don't listen to me" after I warned to chastise him after an incident at school. The humorous part about this incident is that he took off running and I tried to catch him, but he was too fast for me and I was too tired after that to do any type of chastising.

Though I laugh at this now, his words—"Mom, you don't listen to me"—still echo in my ears to this day; they help me to listen and better understand other teenagers and young adults who feel they don't have a voice. Those beautiful words have helped me to become a better listener, single-parent, and community servant leader.

"
But those who wait on the Lord

shall renew their strength; they shall

mount up with wings like eagles;

they shall run and not be weary,
"
they shall walk and not faint.

Isaiah 40:31 (NKJV)

&✦&

Contents

Foreword

This book offers inspiration to young adults everywhere who seek to be the leaders of tomorrow. Just as you are *Predestined to Soar* as a leader of tomorrow, author Una Lisa Williams is a leader of today. Her devotion, drive, and dedication to the Lawton, Fort Sill community is evidenced by her acts of service and accolades of achievement each year, and I am honored to have been asked to compose the foreword of her inspirational book.

As I contemplated writing this foreword, I thought back to my childhood in Lawton. I remember fondly all of the friendships I made while attending Lawton High School and Cameron University. This was an incredibly profound period in my life because I learned so much about working hard to fulfill my personal and professional goals, while striving to aid in the endeavors of others. My lifelong career in public service would soon begin and I reflect on just how much excitement, humility, and passion I felt looking toward the future. There was much to learn, but I was prepared to take on the journey.

And that's what I want to discuss—elements of *your* journey.

No matter who you are or what your beginnings, we need the next generation of thinkers, innovators, and entrepreneurs prepared and focused. Never lose sight of the big picture and your hopes and dreams—of pushing the boundaries for what can be accomplished. You are entrusted with a mission of promoting values of equality, justice, and fairness.

The world today is much more technologically-advanced, culturally-diverse, and socially-accepting than the world that I grew up in as a young man. As globalization and the digital revolution continue to shake the status quo, this generation has the choice to isolate themselves and procrastinate on addressing multifaceted policy challenges, or embrace the future with earnestness and conviction. It is my hope that millennials will choose the latter option.

I believe Una Lisa would also agree with me. After all, this book emphasizes the importance of skills, like embracing life challenges with a positive outlook, changing negative thoughts to positive thoughts, and loving ourselves and others despite any mistakes or wrongdoings. I want to echo Una Lisa's advice that "Now" leaders need to know that no matter what, their voices and aspirations matter. Every millennial has the ability and responsibility to seek opportunities to serve each other. You are never too young to answer the call of public service.

Always be mindful that life truly is about the journey and not the destination. Remember that life is completely non-linear. There may be years of good days, and months of bad, but no matter how challenging or uncertain life becomes, understand there's a beautiful forest through all the trees. Be sure to focus on the big picture for perspective and surround yourself with those who help you to do so.

What ultimately matters is that you love the people around you and that you play some kind of a part in helping to positively impact their lives. Real leaders are servant leaders; fill your circle with people who will challenge you and help you grow each day. Lisa is a servant leader, and she is an excellent role model due to her compassion, dedication, and motivation.

Right now, we need more young, dynamic, and energetic leaders for our community, state, and country. I hope that each of you will consider living a life bigger than yourselves, to serve others with honor and integrity. The challenges we face may seem insurmountable, but with the right attitude and teamwork, your potential to achieve is limitless.

Godspeed.

Fred L. Fitch
Mayor, Lawton, Oklahoma

Acknowledgements

First and foremost, I thank God, Jesus, and the Holy Spirit—my number one team. I learned long ago, "With God all things are possible" (Matthew 19:26, NIV) and "I can do all things through Christ who strengthens me" (Philippians 4:13, NKJV). We had many talks; they provided the guidance and wisdom I needed to write from the heart. They listened to my gripes and complaints, strengthened me to press on, and wiped many tears from my eyes. I could not have done this without them.

I thank my son Matthew T. Taylor (TW), a *mighty man of valor*. Words cannot express how much I love him, through good times and bad, no matter what! He may not believe or think so, but he absolutely helped me make this book a reality. I am extremely proud to be his mom.

I thank my biological mother, Elzena Mae Williams (who is deceased) and my guardian mom, Genevieve B. I thank my two sisters, Christina and Monica; my Auntie's Marjorie, Dora Lee, and Rita; and numerous family members and friends.

I give special thanks to my nephew Kevin B., my niece Ebony B., Angelina B., Cordell W., Margie C. F., Avril W., Debra L., Vivian A., Bobby M., Pastor Ron and Betsy DuPont, my church family at Faith Family Fellowship, Pastor and members of St. Elmo Baptist Church, Mayor Fred L. Fitch, Kathy Monroe, Marty Talley, and last but not least, my Splendor Publishing family. Your support, encouragement, listening ears, and input helped make this inspirational book a success.

Again, and most importantly, I sincerely thank Father God for giving me the strength to achieve as well as the knowledge, skills, experiences, and abilities that He graces me with every day. I credit my life, my son, and all of my accomplishments to Him.

Written for You

Hello, and thank you for allowing me an opportunity to impact your life. Over the years, I have listened to the voices of many young individuals just like you, who feel or believe they are not loved, there is no hope, or that their life, goals, or dreams do not matter. Well I say, "Not so!"

Growing up I experienced the same doubts, and after some time, I learned all those thoughts were not true.

Up front, I want you to know that I am not going to give you a book of intellectual fluff, I am not going to be "preachy," I will not talk *at* you, or just get you momentarily hyped up—no way! Throughout this book you will read about real people and real happenings: no play-play here. This book is written *for* you and dedicated *to* you—personally just for you—yes, *you*! Why? Because your life, goals, dreams, voice, and concerns all matter. You deserve to know that someone has your best interests at heart, believes in you, and desires to assist you in discovering the predestined purpose and plan that was reserved just for you before you were born!

The inspirational moments within these pages are engaging and essential to your life and legacy. You'll have opportunities to reflect, write out positive and healthy solutions, strengthen your confidence, become encouraged, and connect and share with others. You will learn practical strategies and solutions you can apply in your day-to-day-life journey.

Furthermore, this book is about transforming your life and influencing change. It will assist you in renewing your mindset so you can be successful—personally, spiritually, and professionally.

It's time to be valiant, invest in yourself, believe in yourself, uncover your purpose, pursue the desires in your heart, dream big, and build healthy relationships. You will discover how to move forward in the best plans for your life: plans that will prosper you and not harm you; plans that will give you hope and a future (Jeremiah 29:11).

Embrace this book—let it inspire, motivate, encourage, educate, and mostly *empower* you to "Soar" when you encounter one of those unexpected everyday life challenges or obstacles, or when pain tugs at your heart. Only you can change the outcome of your flight! You can soar like an eagle; you were predestined to do great things!

We are in this together, and by stating that I am actually asking you to be engaged. Remember: reflect, write, and even perform some physical activities as you read this book. Your interaction and feedback matter and will contribute to you having a productive, fruitful, and successful life.

So as we journey together, look for the symbol ◀ **ET** ▶ at the end of each chapter.

No, the initials in that symbol do not stand for Extra-Terrestrial, Entertainment Tonight, or Eastern Time; I see you smiling. They stand for ***Engaging Time***. It's our dialog code. During ◀ **ET** ▶ it's okay to smile, laugh, cry, share, take notes . . . oh, and scream! I still do all the above. Invest in this special time just for yourself by setting aside some "*You Time.*" I call it self-care. I recommend at least 30 minutes each day or week; you choose what's best for you.

So let's do a *practice* ◀ **ET** ▶ right now. Can you raise your right hand and shake your head, "Yes"? It's okay to do them both at the same time. Yep, I've got you smiling again. Okay, we are just about ready to start.

The words I will share with you are authentic and come straight from the heart of others and myself. During these inspirational moments we have devoted together, I will pour directly into your mind and heart and provide insight about greater love, greater joy, and greater peace. You are more than worthy of receiving these great things.

Reflect, share, and act. These are important keys to your success in moving forward. Finally, I will speak blessings over you—I will pray for you because I believe that by doing this, you will truly be empowered, encouraged, and reminded that you are not a mistake—oh no, far from it. Your life matters and you are *Predestined to Soar*!

What you need to know *right now*, at this moment in your life—whether you are facing a challenge or getting ready to celebrate another achievement—no matter what is going on or where you are, is that God loves you. You are purposefully and wonderfully made, there is hope, you are not a failure, you matter greatly, and you can climb high. God has the best life plan for you and now is the time for you to take care of your destiny and tap into the purpose you were placed on this beautiful earth to accomplish. He wants you to walk into victory.

You may be thinking, "It's too late for me." Nope, it is *not* too late. I am a living testament of that fact, and throughout this inspirational book, I will share true stories of other young men and women just like you, who felt the same way but who are now working toward their *predestined plan and purpose*.

Yes, it's true that sometimes you will not choose wisely and you will face challenges or hit a bump in the road—hey, who hasn't? I surely did, many times. So before you think or say "She doesn't understand," or before you think that I do not "feel ya," all I ask is that you remember this about me: I was once your age! I have been serving in the community as a youth and young adult leader since junior high school. I've "been there" and still go through "valleys," and I know I will face more trials and tribulations again. However, I keep moving forward.

These words will deepen your desire to press beyond whatever "weapons" that will form against you. These obstacles and concerns may show up in your life and try to stress you out:

- *getting passing grades in school*
- *being rejected by a social group*
- *not being able to go on a fun trip with friends*
- *wondering if you will get a date for your prom*
- *worrying about having food to eat at home*
- *getting teased for wearing the same clothes as last year*
- *being bullied because you have a handicap*
- *wondering if you'll succeed because your mom or dad is not in your life*
- *being able to purchase the cap and gown you need to walk across the stage for your graduation*
- *getting through the mounds of paperwork in order to go to college*

Good news: you don't have to panic. Continue to breathe because 1) you are not alone, and 2) I will give you great tools for your "life's tool box" during our time together.

Ok, ◀ ET ▶ again: I need you to pinch or poke yourself right now. You feel a little bit of pain, right? That's another reminder that you are still alive and better days are coming. You have been given another chance to do better for yourself. This is your opportunity to be a responsible, productive, and positive influence in your community.

BEFORE WE BEGIN

I know you are excited about diving into your new engaging, inspirational, and empowering book, but before we do, a couple of things must be done.

Why? Because *you* are the center of attention and all eyes must be on *you* during this time, so let's set the stage. Only *you* can make this happen. I ask that you seriously complete these first couple of exercises and do this every time before getting started with each chapter reading.

◀ET▶

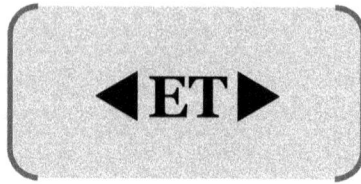

SET THE STAGE BEFORE YOU READ EACH CHAPTER

1. Eliminate of all distractions: no phone (absolutely a no-no), no TV, no video games, no snacking (okay, maybe a little water), no computer, and no electronics during our quality time. You could even make a sign that reads, *"Me-Time in Session: Will Hail You Up Later"* (something one of my island friends would say before departing).

2. Go to a mirror and look yourself in the eyes. Place your hand over your heart—oh, and you must do this with a smile on your face for this exercise to be effective; I see you smiling already—great start. Say this as loud as you can:

   > *"I love me, I am loved unconditionally, I am valuable, I am not forgotten, I am courageous, fear is not my friend, I am determined, there is hope for me and my dreams, there is a purpose for me being here on this earth, I am not a mistake, confidence is my strength, I am already fearfully and wonderfully made, I will 'let no one despise my youth,' and furthermore, I believe in myself—no matter what others may think or say."*

Wow! Give yourself a hand-clap. You see, these are positive power words that will bring joy to your life every day. They will help you move forward when faced with a challenge and lead you into the victory that you so much deserve.

This is not about being perfect, but about tapping into the perfection that the Creator of all has so graciously implanted into you. New beginnings start now, so don't let the *should've* or *could've* mentality stop you.

Here we go. Lets' get started!

❧ ✦ ☙

My Personal Notes: _____

_____

_____

_____

_____

_____

_____

_____

_____

_____

_____

_____

_____

_____

_____

_____

_____

_____

_____

_____

_____

_____

≈✦≈

Chapter 1

You are Loved Unconditionally

Without a shadow of doubt, you are loved unconditionally by the One who created all humans and this world. It doesn't matter what you have done or what negative things you may have said to yourself or to others. Even if you have been rebellious and disrespectful, or done things you feel ashamed of or guilty about, God wants you to know He loves you unconditionally.

With that stated, not all words or actions are healthy for your life. Please do not let the negative thoughts that run through your head or the actions of others deceive you into thinking otherwise. His love will never change towards you.

There are no "ifs" when it comes to His genuine love . . . the love that never fails! He loves you just the way you are—even through your mistakes—and with open arms He is always available to embrace you with His marvelous love. The Creator sets no boundaries or limits when it comes to His love for you. He never makes you feel unwanted and He never does anything to harm you. He also does not require you to act in a certain way to receive His unconditional love. God is love gentle!

His unconditional love *never* looks like this:

"If" you love me you will buy this for me.

"If" you love me you will wear this outfit for me.

"If" you love me you will sneak out.

"If" you love me you will do this certain act.

"If" you love me you will cheat for me.

I could go on and on about what real love does *not* look like. But instead, I truly need you to focus on the Creator's unconditional love that He has just for you.

Love should never come with any conditions imposed on you by someone who says they love you. You should never have to prove your love to someone by doing something they think you should do. Nope, that's not the right way and it surely is not love; those types of acts are actually selfish!

Deep down inside, I don't think you are cool or comfortable with doing anything you know is a "no go." I know . . . been there, done that, and in the end I had no joy or peace, and life was passing me by quickly; I was mainly living someone else's life. And after speaking with many young people, I discovered that a lot of you feel the same way and have had similar experiences: doing things only to make someone love or like you, or to belong, or to be a part of a certain click or group.

So, think about this: when you decide not to follow the Creator's plans for your life, when you decide not to love and serve others, when you decide to stop attending church, when you choose to ignore the Creator's loving commands because they seem old-school or ancient to you, guess what? He still loves you unconditionally. Now, the things mentioned above happen to be very healthy for you and can be beneficial; they will help you create a great life. So think about adding these activities to your life, or look into other positive outlets and link up. Just remember you are still loved.

I hope you will take note of all the things I just shared, and remember, this is not about me preaching at or to you; this is about sharing what's best for you so you can move forward in life. This is about you becoming a productive and purposeful individual for yourself and your community. It's about you knowing that the Creator's love is unconditional.

The Creator loves you, and He is a total gentlemen.

Remember, whenever you hear the word "if," it's all about the other person's feelings and that's called "conditional love." Love that is given freely without any strings attached is called "unconditional love." It is the love that comes to us from the Creator, and at times throughout your life you will receive this type of love from others. Welcome it. You are worth receiving unconditional love.

◀ET▶

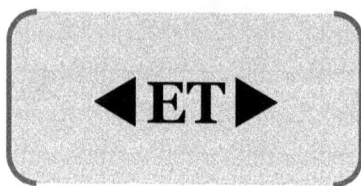

REFLECT, WRITE, TAKE ACTION

1. Reflect on what you read:

   What stands out to you?

   Do you believe you are loved unconditionally by the Creator or by others?

   Share your thoughts and experiences, good or bad.

   Would you be willing to share your thoughts with others to express how you feel or to make a situation better? If not, why?

   Are there areas in your life where you are asked to compromise? If so, how do you feel about that? What actions will you take for yourself to get out of it?

2. Reach out to at least three people (one family member, one friend, and one acquaintance). Share with them the difference between unconditional love and conditional love. Challenge them to do the same—keep it going.

   Journal the responses (write them in a notebook).

SCRIPTURE: 1 Corinthians 13: 4-8 (NIV)

"Love is patient, love is kind. It does not envy, it does not boast, it is not proud. It does not dishonor others, it is not self-seeking, it is not easily angered, it keeps no record of wrongs. Love does not delight in evil but rejoices with the truth. It always protects, always trusts, always hopes, always perseveres."

PRAYER

Father God, thank You for Your child who is reading this prayer. Just like You have proven Your unconditional love to me so many times, even when I have made mistakes or compromised based on the wants of others and their "love of conditions," I ask You to manifest Your unconditional love to Your child reading this prayer. Thank You Father God, for Your continued protection, provision, guidance, and grace. Thank You for the love You give unconditionally in spite of where we are in life, what we did in the past, or any upcoming mistakes, in Jesus' name, amen.

❧ ✦ ☙

My Personal Notes: _____

_____

_____

_____

_____

_____

_____

_____

_____

_____

_____

_____

_____

_____

_____

_____

_____

_____

_____

_____

_____

_____

�✦⋪

Chapter 2

Endure:
Keep Swimming

Sometimes a goal will seem too much to bear. Florence Chadwick is known for long distance open water swimming. In short, she attempted to swim 26 miles but was faced with a few challenges: concerns about being attacked by sharks, interference from boats floating around, thick fog, and the thought of becoming tired.

Just like Florence, you may doubt your abilities, but you must persevere. Keep swimming, do not quit, the end may be closer than you think.

Well, Florence did quit and later discovered she was one mile away for her destination!

When you are faced with obstacles that may try to block you from finishing what you set out to do, you have to "keep your eyes on the prize."

When I was going through some military training during cold, wet, and muggy days, I laughed, cried, prayed, and thought about a better life for my son and me. I had to endure those temporary moments of obstacles and "keep swimming."

Remember that you have a goal to complete and that challenges are only temporary; don't stop swimming. Winning and losing make up only a small percentage of what matters. The higher percentage is that you tried your best, tried something new, and kept swimming.

Florence did try again and she completed her goal—she stayed focused. So whether the end result comes out in your favor or not, endure for the moment—keep swimming!

◀ET▶

REFLECT, WRITE, TAKE ACTION

1. Think of a goal that you find challenging right now which requires you to endure—to "keep swimming."

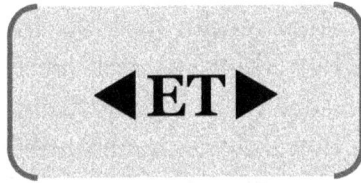

   What healthy things can you do to "keep your eyes on the prize"? Some examples might be to think about a happy place, listen to your favorite victory song, or treat yourself to your favorite snack.

2. Reach out to at least three people (one family member, one friend, and one acquaintance) who may need your help to keep swimming. Share with each other a few "keep swimming" ideas.

   Journal the responses.

SCRIPTURE: Galatians 6: 9 (NIV)

   "Let us not become weary in doing good, for at the proper time we will reap a harvest if we do not give up."

PRAYER

   Father God, thank You for Your child who is reading this prayer. I am asking that You show them how

17

to build up their endurance so they can keep swimming. Help them to not let challenges or obstacles pressure them into quitting. Father God, remind them that they are not alone—You are there with them and they can call out to You anytime for strength. Thank You for helping them meet the goals they set out to complete, in Jesus' name, amen.

❧ ✦ ☙

My Personal Notes: _____

_____

_____

_____

_____

_____

_____

_____

_____

_____

_____

_____

_____

_____

_____

_____

_____

_____

_____

_____

_____

_____

_____

_____

_____

_____

❧ ✦ ❧

Chapter 3

Not Forgotten:
You are Too Valuable

You must know that you are valuable and not forgotten. Yes, sometimes things in life may seem a little bleak, however, there will always be someone who is placed in your path at just the right time to help guide you and provide you with the tools and resources you need.

I had the pleasure of meeting a beautiful young lady—I will call her Lady JP—who attended our Family and Friend reunion with her parents.

The moment I decided to engage Lady JP, I knew this was another opportunity for me to help someone move forward in the predestined purpose and plan the Creator had already mapped out for their life.

Our conversation was mostly about her interests, desires, and future, and she shared with me her discouragement with preparing for college.

The few things I felt led to share with her immediately perked her up, and she stated, "That is good to know." She was supposed to be having fun at the event, enjoying all the great home-cooked Louisiana soul and sea food, not focusing on college challenges.

I agreed to stay in contact with her, but it was a few weeks before I reached out to her to let her know she was not forgotten. She responded, "OMG 👏 👏 👏, I thought I was forgotten about." This actually brought joy to my heart. I then reassured her that she was not forgotten and I reminded her of how valuable she is. I assured her that all would turn out well. This is also my word to you. Though it may feel like it at times, you must understand that God's timing is perfect. You are not forgotten—you are too valuable.

◀ ET ▶

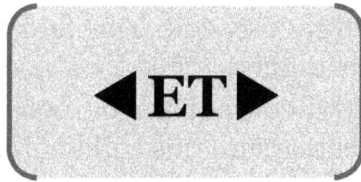

REFLECT, WRITE, TAKE ACTION

1. Reflect on a couple of times when you felt forgotten.

    How did you respond?

    Did you reach out to anyone? What was the end result?

    What could you do differently next time, if the end result was negative?

2. Reach out to at least three people (one family member, one friend, and one acquaintance) and let them know they are not forgotten. Remind them of how valuable they are in this life.

    Journal the responses.

SCRIPTURE: Mathew 10:31 (NKJV)

"Do not fear therefore; you are of more value than many sparrows."

PRAYER

Father God, thank You for Your child who is reading this prayer. Just like You said, the sparrows are not forgotten before You, and You faithfully remind us that we are of more value than many sparrows. You said You will never leave or forsake us, and so I ask that You reassure this child of that. Let them know deep in their heart that they are not forgotten. Remind them of how valuable they are to You and to this world, in Jesus' name, amen.

My Personal Notes: _____

_____

_____

_____

_____

_____

_____

_____

_____

_____

_____

_____

_____

_____

_____

_____

_____

_____

_____

_____

_____

_____

_____

_____

_____

એ✦ણ

Chapter 4

Fearfully and Wonderfully Made

You cannot be duplicated. No! Nope, nope, nope. Nope—you are unique!

I was having a discussion with a close military buddy who has a genuine love for all children. He stated, "I believe that our young ones are inundated on a daily basis with negative, gutter-nonsense and are being taught that everything good is bad and the movie-star look is the thing. They are being stripped of true beauty and the meaning of dignity . . . don't get me started." (That's just too funny.)

When you look at yourself in the mirror and see that you don't look like someone else, that's a *good* thing. Why do you want your true beauty to be altered? When you desire to look like someone else you are no longer modeling *your* unique image, but someone else's. You are *already* beautiful; you are already handsome.

You were specially made with your one-of-a-kind image to match your personality, which will bless many others. You are special. The world's opinion on how you should look should never matter; worrying about it will only bring you dissatisfaction, confusion, and pain. You were fearfully and wonderfully made by the Creator of all and He does not make mistakes.

◀ ET ▶

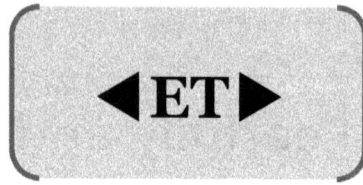

REFLECT, REFLECT, WRITE, TAKE ACTION

1. Think about a couple of times when you changed your appearance for someone or to look like someone else.

   How did you feel after making those changes (sad, didn't really want to, felt you were doing it to please them, etc.).

   Now think of positive ways to respond to someone who feels that you need to change your look. What positive words will you say to yourself when you want to change your unique image? Write at least three responses.

2. Reach out to at least three people (one family member, one friend, and one acquaintance) who may possibly be struggling in this area and share something positive with them.

   Yep, journal the responses.

SCRIPTURE: Psalm 139:14 (NIV)

"I praise You because I am fearfully and wonderfully made; Your works are wonderful, I know that full well."

PRAYER

Heavenly Father, thank You for the "fearfully and wonderfully made" child who is reading this prayer. Thank You that they now realize that You uniquely created them, and that the world's opinion (whether family, friend, or stranger) of how they should look is just that—their *opinion*. Thank You that Your child now accepts and embraces their unique image. Thank You for giving them positive ways to respond to negative influences, in Jesus name, amen!

❧ ✦ ☙

My Personal Notes: _____

_____

_____

_____

_____

_____

_____

_____

_____

_____

_____

_____

_____

_____

_____

_____

_____

_____

_____

_____

_____

_____

❧ ✦ ☙

Chapter 5

Believe in You:
Move Forward

Believing in yourself starts with you. Before you were born, dreams, gifts, and talents were placed in your heart by the Creator. There may be times you feel inadequate to achieve a goal or birth the dreams you have envisioned. Listen up . . . believe in you and move forward!

You maybe despised because of your youth, but the Creator tells us in His word to not let anyone despise you because of your youth. Different varieties of rejection may come from friends, family, community leaders, and even church people— hey, that's okay. Maintain your dignity and respect with them anyway. Obey your parents always. Invest in yourself! When you get a burning desire to do something, go for it.

Critics will always be there, and they will never understand you or be *for* you. Just let them push you on into your purpose. Gain resources, connect with other visionaries who speak your language, and build your "life's toolbox." Do what you need to do to positively—and in a healthy way—make whatever it is you are looking towards, happen.

Once again I am here to tell you that you are not alone; I have been there, and I still struggle at times with the same feelings you do. Yep, even at my age—(which I will not share— well, not yet). Before you were created, you were equipped by your Creator to accomplish what is making your heart so excited and your mind fill with wonder. Remember to start the journey by believing in yourself, and keep moving forward.

"A dream doesn't become reality through magic; it takes sweat, determination, and hard work."

-Colin Powell

◀ET▶

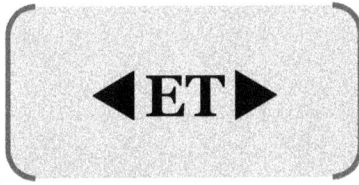

REFLECT, WRITE, TAKE ACTION

1. Think of areas in your life where you have stopped believing in yourself and stopped moving forward.

   What are some positive healthy plans you can do to change that?

   Who can you reach out to who could help you?

2. Reach out to at least three people (one family member, one friend, and one acquaintance) who may possibly be struggling in this area. Share ideas and resources to help them believe in themselves and keep moving forward no matter what.

   Journal the responses.

SCRIPTURE: Jeremiah 29:11 (NIV)

> "'For I know the plans I have for you,' declares the Lord, 'plans to prosper you and not to harm you, plans to give you hope and a future.'"

PRAYER

Father God, thank You for Your child who is reading this prayer and for showing them the dreams, gifts, and talents You placed in their heart. Thank You for ordering their steps as they work towards fulfilling their goals and dreams. Help them to share with others in their community, in Jesus' name, amen.

My Personal Notes: _____

_____

_____

_____

_____

_____

_____

_____

_____

_____

_____

_____

_____

_____

_____

_____

_____

_____

_____

_____

_____

_____

_____

_____

_____

❧ ✦ ❧

Chapter 6

Fear is a Liar

When we hear or see something that feels powerful to us in our journey, we grip it and apply it. When I heard the song "Fear is a Liar" by one of my favorite musical artists, I thought, "So true!" Here are some of the lyrics to the song:

> *"When he told you you're not good enough,*
> *When he told you you're not right,*
> *When he told you you're not strong enough,*
> *To put up a good fight,*
> *When he told you you're not worthy,*
> *When he told you you're not loved,*
> *When he told you you're not beautiful,*
> *That you'll never be enough*
>
> *Fear he is a liar . . . "*

-Lyrics from "Fear is a Liar," by Zach Williams

I totally agree.

These same words were being echoed years ago as I was watching an old western episode; one cowboy shouted to another cowboy, "You are worthless and no good." The second cowboy just ignored the first one, and by doing so he proved to himself that he was not worthless. You may realize already that words like these are lies, but still they can affect you if you let them. I highly encourage you to *not* allow fear to block you from enjoying life, receiving your blessings, and moving forward in any area of your life. Fear *is* a liar. It does not want you to win; it tries to make you miss out on the beauty of life.

◀ **ET** ▶

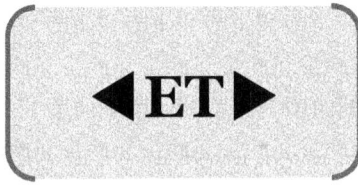

REFLECT, WRITE, TAKE ACTION

1. Think—I mean seriously *think*; are there any areas in your life right now where fear is in the way?

    Write them down by listing them like this:

    "This is what fear tells me . . ."

    Then, say this to that fear, "I am fearless, energetic, amazing, and radiant!" Now, what are you going to do to positively and in a healthy way kick fear to the curb (by the way, FEAR stands for False Evidence Appearing Real)?

2. Reach out to at least three people (one family member, one friend, and one acquaintance) who may possibly be struggling in this area. Share with them what fear is and is not.

    Journal the responses.

SCRIPTURE: 2 Timothy 1:7 (NKJV)

> "For God has not given us a spirit of fear, but of power and of love and of a sound mind."

PRAYER

Father God, thank You for your child who is reading this prayer. Thank You that they no longer have the spirit of fear, but peace, joy, and a sound mind. They are set free from the lie of fear and they now declare that they are *fearless, energetic, amazing,* and *radiant*, in Jesus' name, amen.

❧✦☙

My Personal Notes: _____

_____

_____

_____

_____

_____

_____

_____

_____

_____

_____

_____

_____

_____

_____

_____

_____

_____

_____

_____

_____

_____

_____

_____

❧ ✦ ☙

Chapter 7

The Confidence in You

The young beauty queen shared, "I listened to my boyfriend and others tell me I would not do well because I stutter and stumble over my words." Well, for some time this young lady *did* listen to these hurtful words, but finally she built up her confidence, got help with her speech impairment, and later participated in a beauty pageant . . . and she *won*! Yes! She now speaks at seminars and shares her story, and she is only sixteen years old. Oh, and she left that so called "boyfriend" alone—"Nobody got time for that!"

Confidence is already in you; activate it and "walk it out." Take the challenge—and if you stumble, try again. Each time I have to speak in front of a hundred or more military folks, I pray and breathe. If I don't, nervousness starts to tug at me and the confidence I have inside tries to hide. Nope, *not* happening. I truly believe most of us struggle in this way because we don't find ways to overcome this temporary obstacle.

Don't let anyone tell you who you are—that you *can't* do it or that you're not going to do well. Know who you are and don't settle for low self-esteem; you have important things to do, and you just don't like boring stuff! Tap into the confidence already in you and breathe. You are more than a conqueror.

◀ ET ▶

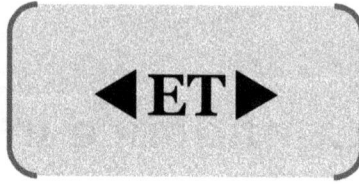

REFLECT, WRITE, TAKE ACTION

1. In which areas of your life have you lost confidence in yourself?

   What can you do to overcome?

2. Reach out to at least three people (one family member, one friend, and one acquaintance) who may possibly be struggling in this area. Discuss ways you overcame and ask them what they can do and if you can help them in any way.

   Yep, journal the experience/responses.

SCRIPTURE: Romans 8:37 (NIV)

> *"No, in all these things we are more than conquerors through Him who loved us."*

PRAYER

Father God, thank You for Your child who is reading this prayer. Thank You for reminding them that they are more than a conquer, with You *all* things are possible, and they can overcome the struggle with confidence. Thank You Father for helping them find the healthy resources they need. Place the right people in their path to assist them, in Jesus' name, amen.

❦✦❧

My Personal Notes: _____

_____

_____

_____

_____

_____

_____

_____

_____

_____

_____

_____

_____

_____

_____

_____

_____

_____

_____

_____

_____

_____

❧ ✦ ❧

Chapter 8

Be Courageous:
Tell Your Own Story

One afternoon while I was in my office, a young soldier man came to drop of some paperwork. He was very polite but he seemed a little shy and tense. I asked how he was doing, and not knowing his current situation, I inquired about his future after the military.

A little taken back by my question, he had a surprised and shocked look on his face. He began to share that he didn't know, but he had a couple of ideas. Further into the conversation, I learned about his interests, where he was from, and most importantly, that he was facing an early discharge—something he was not looking forward to—because he desired to continue to serve.

Without being nosey or seeming to pry, I wanted to know what he was planning on doing about his situation, but he was not sure anything could be done because he believed, "It is what it is." But because I believed it was not by chance that he was in my office, and that it was a divine appointment, I shared with him an opportunity I knew of that could help him. I felt in my heart that it would truly benefit him.

I recommended that he use the Commander's Open Door Policy and speak on his own behalf. Well, he really did not like that idea because he thought he was not worthy of the commander's time, and from what he heard through the grapevine, there was no hope for him. That put a big dent in his courage.

After a little pep talk, I said, "Be courageous—tell your own story, tell him your desires; I believe he wants to hear from you. Get on his calendar."

Before leaving my office, he said, "Ms. Williams, you just don't know. I was feeling lower than low, lower than rock bottom, and I didn't know what I was going to do (he was in tears).

It took him about a week before building up the courage. In the end, victory rang in his heart. His posture changed, and he is still serving in the military and doing great things (now tears are dropping from *my* eyes. Yep, I don't mind shedding tears—they are joyful).

I don't believe you want a hand out but a hand *up,* and to be given another chance. But remember, you must act on it. Speak up for yourself. Tell your story (clearly, respectfully, and professionally) even when you believe you are standing by yourself or feel all alone. Never let negative "noise" dirty up your ears. Use those words to affect positive change for your life, and always give the person who has to make the final decision a chance—when the opportunity is there. Your voice matters and makes a big difference. Be courageous and never be afraid to tell your own story; many times that's all it takes.

◀ **ET** ▶

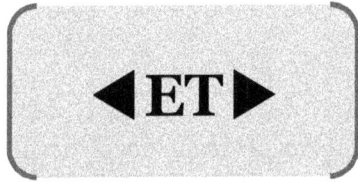

REFLECT, WRITE, TAKE ACTION

1. Are there situations in your life where you could build up your courage and *go for it*?

    What actions can you take, such as write someone a letter, meet with the teacher after class, get help with that college application, or speak to someone?

    What will it take to clear the air and move you away from stressing over it?

2. Reach out to at least three people (one family member, one friend, and one acquaintance) and ask them if they are willing to share a situation they are struggling with in this area, where courage does not seem to be on their side. Share your story and the benefits of being courageous and telling your own story.

    Journal the responses.

SCRIPTURE: Deuteronomy 31:6 (NKJV)

> *"Be strong and of good courage, do not fear nor be afraid of them; for the Lord your God, He is the one who goes with you. He will not leave you nor forsake you."*

PRAYER

Father God, thank You for Your child who is reading this prayer. I ask that they learn through Your love, that they are more than conquerors. I thank You that they will be strong and let their heart take courage. They will not be frightened or dismayed because You are with them wherever they go, in Jesus' name, amen.

❧✦❧

My Personal Notes: _____

_____

_____

_____

_____

_____

_____

_____

_____

_____

_____

_____

_____

_____

_____

_____

_____

_____

_____

_____

_____

_____

_____

ରେ ✦ ରେ

Chapter 9

Maintain Respect Anyway

I know at times someone will say or do something to hurt you but I believe you know how to maintain your own dignity and respect in spite of it. When you do that, you demonstrate respect for yourself and you teach those around you—including the one who disrespected you—that responding disrespectfully is just not cool.

No, you are not being a coward, sissy, scaredy-cat, or any such thing when you respond with dignity. Instead, you have chosen a positive, healthy way to make a great impact. Yes, you deserve to be respected; however, you are the key to making this world a better place. Responding positively when you have been disrespected reaps loving, peaceful, and healthy benefits.

I have always taught my son that no matter what people say, don't be disrespectful, and yes, I know that's a challenge. But I have gotten many reports from others, both young and old, who shared with me how they witnessed my son applying my teachings.

Do the right thing, not the "normal" thing or what you may have learned to do or what you may have seen others do.

You may hear, "If they disrespect me, I will disrespect them right back," or "If you want to be respected, you have to earn it," or "Respect is not just given." Well, I have to say, I don't agree. From experience, when I used to think that way, I really did not feel good about it. But when I respected anyway, I felt good and many people would either come back and apologize, or say something like, "Man, I don't know if I could have taken that but I am glad you did not act the same way as they did." Whether it's your parents, co-workers, supervisor, classmate, or a stranger who comes at you sideways, maintain dignity and respect; it will benefit you in the long run and add to a longer life.

The will of our Creator is for us to show respect to everyone. Being respectful—no matter what life throws at you—goes a long way.

◀ **ET** ▶

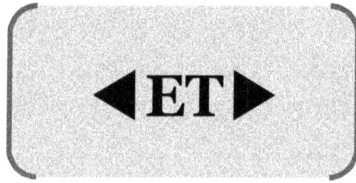

REFLECT, WRITE, TAKE ACTION

1. Have you had experience with the disrespectful bug?

   What happened, how did you respond, and how did you feel afterwards?

   How would you respond next time?

2. Reach out to at least three people (one family member, one friend, and one acquaintance) who you can either go back to and get it right with (apologize), or share with about the advantages of not being disrespectful under any circumstances.

   Journal the responses.

SCRIPTURE: 1 Peter 2:17 13: 4-8 (NIV)

"Show proper respect to everyone, love the family of believers . . . ."

PRAYER

Father God, thank You for Your child who is reading this prayer. I ask You to help them set an example by doing what is good and showing integrity. I pray they show proper respect to everyone and "love anyway." Thank You Father God that they are not showing weakness but a display of humility, in Jesus' name, amen.

᪥✦᪥

My Personal Notes: _____

_____

_____

_____

_____

_____

_____

_____

_____

_____

_____

_____

_____

_____

_____

_____

_____

_____

_____

_____

_____

_____

_____

_____

_____

_____

❧✦❧

Chapter 10

Living Hopeful

Where there is a will, there is a way—exceptions are out there.

Remember, I shared with you that you are too valuable. Trials and tribulations can truly stretch your sense of hope, and sometimes you just don't see the end of the tunnel. Keep in mind that you are not alone in your walk. Look around, there *is* help, and things *will* get better; live hopeful.

Even when it seems for a moment that there is no hope: you learn you may not graduate, many teens and young adults are dying prematurely, you see abuse all around you, your best friend was diagnosed with a sickness that left them bed bound, and the list can go on and on. I want you to know *there is hope*.

Each day you are awakened into this beautiful "land of the living," you have been given another chance to create hope for yourself and others. Hope often comes when you reflect just a little, like when you realize things *did* work out even though a few days ago you saw no hope. Most importantly though, hope springs forth from how you respond to the everyday drama that's all around you. Hope becomes lost when we do nothing. Hope actually grows when you do your best to make things happen, even in the midst of "it all." Know that each time you take a positive step you are living hopeful.

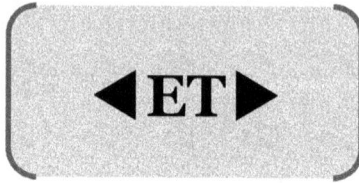

◀ **ET** ▶

REFLECT, WRITE, TAKE ACTION

1. Think about some of the things going on around you and in your local community that may seem hopeless. How can you contribute to showing others that living hopeful is the best route to take?

2. Reach out to at least three people (one family member, one friend, and one acquaintance) and find out what they think about living hopeful. Ask if they have any ideas on how they can encourage others to live hopeful.

   Journal the responses.

SCRIPTURE: Romans 12:12 (NKJV)

   "Rejoicing in hope, patient in tribulation, continuing steadfastly in prayer."

PRAYER

Father God, thank You for Your child who is reading this prayer. Thank You for showing them how living hopeful means we hope in Christ, and that they really do have hope in this life. Help them not to "lose heart," and show them that if they hope for what they do not see, You will help them to wait for it with patience. Father, thank You that they can rejoice in hope, be patient in tribulations, and be constant in prayer, in Jesus' name, amen.

❧ ✦ ☙

My Personal Notes: _____

_____

_____

_____

_____

_____

_____

_____

_____

_____

_____

_____

_____

_____

_____

_____

_____

_____

_____

_____

_____

_____

_____

❧✦❧

Chapter 11

Start by Forgiving

Forgiveness can be a hard pill to swallow when it comes to forgiving ourselves or others. Either way, when we don't forgive—like a bad disease—it will slowly eat our insides, and before long, our outside appearance looks like a disease! Do not think you cannot forgive yourself or others. It's possible. It all boils down to what your life means to you.

No one is perfect! We all have and will make mistakes and we will mess up. Do not beat yourself up; just get that thing behind you so you don't miss out on life. Yea, I hear you, "You don't know what I did, you don't know what I said, I feel so bad, I can't face it." I am here to tell you this: first, forgive yourself, and then if the opportunity is presented to you, go back and make it right, then *let it go*.

There is nothing you have done that says it's over for you—it's the end of life. Remember, you are not alone. This is life, it happens, move forward, it's okay. There were times I would beat myself up about forgiving myself and others. Well let me tell you, it made me sick; socializing with others was a challenge; my eating habits unnecessarily cost me a lot of money; my clothes needed a couple of downgrades in size because I had stopped eating; I was grumpy with other folks; and I began to look scary to myself and others. Then, I started thinking, "Unforgiveness is not a good thing. Enough is enough. I have to get it together."

My choices for coping were not healthy—I had to start forgiving myself. I had to apologize/ask forgiveness. Oh, and I had to *not blame* others.

But I'll tell you, before I got it right, it was eating me up inside and showing on the outside. Don't let an issue marinate in your mind or heart. Just know that everyone experiences this. The bottom line is to quickly forgive yourself and do what you can to make it right; delaying it will only make it worse. Yep, it may seem hard but it's the best and right thing to do, and you *will* be okay!

◀ET▶

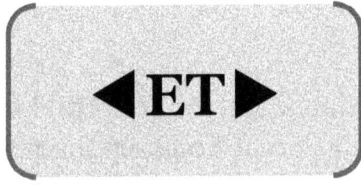

REFLECT, WRITE, TAKE ACTION

1. How many times have you faced a situation pertaining to forgiveness? Can you think of someone you can forgive?

   What plan of action will you take: write them a note, send them a text, or take some face-to-face time to forgive them, or forgive yourself and perhaps even let them forgive you? Focus on moving forward and doing your part—it will be alright in the end.

2. Reach out to as many people as possible (family members, friends, acquaintances) to start a "Forgiving Revolution." Share with others the importance of forgiving. You can do this! Think of how you are making the world better.

   Journal the responses.

SCRIPTURE: Colossians 3:13 (NIV)

"Bear with each other and forgive one another if any of you has a grievance against someone. Forgive as the Lord forgave you."

PRAYER

Father God, thank You for Your child who is reading this prayer. I ask that You help them with peaceful resolutions. Father, You said for us to forgive other people when they sin against us and You will also forgive us. Help them to forgive. Thank You for showing them that this too shall pass, in Jesus' name, amen.

❧ ✦ ☙

My Personal Notes: _____

_____

_____

_____

_____

_____

_____

_____

_____

_____

_____

_____

_____

_____

_____

_____

_____

_____

_____

_____

_____

_____

_____

❧✦☙

Chapter 12

Chosen: Nope, You are Not a Mistake

Okay, lookie here, beautiful person. You have been *chosen*—nope, you are *not* a mistake. Just think about what the world would be like if you were not in it.

The Creator knew you would be a great fit and there is nothing you have done or said that can change that.

Life will bring disappointments. It may throw the whole kitchen sink at you and the living room, too, and you may not know what to do. It's okay. None of us came out of the womb instantly making great things happen, but the very fact that *you happened* is a huge blessing in itself.

Now, don't get me wrong. Great things have been imbedded inside of you by the Creator of all. Sometimes it just takes a while for us to tap in, you got that?

So even though a parent is not in your life, someone didn't pick you to be on their team, you are not yet able to get the clothes you like, or you don't yet have a date for the dance, you are still chosen and you are not a mistake.

Sometimes life takes a little time to catch up with others, not necessarily with you. Someone may want to pick you for the team but may realize you are better off helping another team. And if a parent is not in your life, don't ever think you are a mistake; life may have to catch up with them (sometimes it does and sometimes it does not). Regardless, you are still loved, valuable, chosen, and not a mistake. You have it in you to show the world how to do it better. And yes, I see you smiling!

69

◀ET▶

REFLECT, WRITE, TAKE ACTION

1. Do you sometimes think you are a mistake? How do you feel about that and how is it affecting your life?

   What can you do to help yourself get out from those negative feelings?

2. Reach out to as many individuals in your age group as you can and find out their thoughts on feeling like they are not chosen and believing they are a mistake. Come up with some healthy coping mechanisms to help you or them to let it go.

   Journal the experience.

SCRIPTURE: Psalm 139:13-17 (NIV)

"For You created my inmost being; You knit me together in my mother's womb. I praise You because I am fearfully and wonderfully made; Your works are wonderful, I know that full well. My frame was not hidden from You when I was made in the secret place, when I was woven together in the depths of the earth. Your eyes saw my unformed body; all the days ordained for me were written in Your book before one of

them came to be. How precious to me are your thoughts, God! How vast is the sum of them!

PRAYER

Father God, thank You for Your child who is reading this prayer. Show them that they are a heritage and that You chose them, and they are not a mistake. Thank You for never leaving them, especially when they go through life's challenges. Show them that they are needed on this earth to help make things better, in Jesus' name, amen.

❧ ✦ ☙

My Personal Notes: _____

_____

_____

_____

_____

_____

_____

_____

_____

_____

_____

_____

_____

_____

_____

_____

_____

_____

_____

_____

_____

_____

❧ ✦ ☙

Chapter 13

Be Resilient

Wow, it just happened: you failed an important test, locked yourself out of the house (and mom can't leave work), had a car incident, lost the game because you didn't make that shot for the team. How can you bounce back from this?

Sometimes we win and sometimes we lose, however, life must go on. Learn from the thing that just happened and use it as a growing tool, or use it to encourage someone else, but you must move on. If not, life will pass you by before you know it, and you will realize you cannot go back and change what happened, it's too late. Don't dwell on that mistake and don't let others make you feel regretful; I am sure there were times in life when they experienced failures, too.

"Tough times never last, but tough people do."

-Robert H. Schuller

All things are possible. You can and will bounce back. I once saw a church sign that read, "Life is not a remote control—you have to get up and change it." That speaks volumes, and only you can make that change in your life. Be Resilient!

"It's hard to beat a person who never gives up."

-George Herman Ruth, Jr. (The Babe)

◀ ET ▶

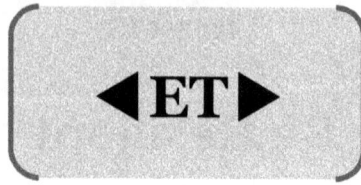

REFLECT, WRITE, TAKE ACTION

1. Reflect on recent experiences where you have had to be resilient and "bounce back" quickly in order to keep moving. Was that hard for you to do?

   Consider some things you could say to yourself or even do that would help you to bounce back—that is, be resilient—when a situation in life requires it.

2. Reach out to at least three people (one family member, one friend, and one acquaintance) and ask them what their main strategies are for bouncing back after a setback. If they do not have specific practices, offer suggestions for healthy strategies related to being resilient that you can all benefit from.

   Journal the responses.

SCRIPTURE: Romans 8:28 (NKJV)

> *"And we know that all things work together for good to those who love God, to those who are the called according to His purpose.*

PRAYER

Father God, thank You for Your child who is reading this prayer. Help them to know they do not have to be afraid or panic. Speak to them that all things will work together for their good. Thank You Father that they are resilient and as they look to You, nothing will mess up Your plan for them. Help them not to let any negative words stop them from bouncing back, in Jesus' name, amen.

❧ ✦ ☙

My Personal Notes: _____

_____

_____

_____

_____

_____

_____

_____

_____

_____

_____

_____

_____

_____

_____

_____

_____

_____

_____

_____

_____

_____

_____

_____

❧ ✦ ☙

Chapter 14

My Declaration

I am a

Young Lady of Worth / Mighty Man of Valor!
I am loved and valued.
I am "fearfully and wonderfully made."
I have a purpose in life.
I am fearless, energetic, amazing, and resilient!
I am seizing opportunities to be educated,
equipped, and empowered.
I can effectively voice my concerns, pursue my
dreams, and reach my goals.
I am writing out my visions and making them plain.
I am overcoming challenges and breaking barriers.
I choose healthy relationships.
I connect with NOW leaders and help pave the way
for FUTURE leaders.
I am *Predestined to Soar*!

❧✦☙

My Personal Notes: _____

_____

_____

_____

_____

_____

_____

_____

_____

_____

_____

_____

_____

_____

_____

_____

_____

_____

_____

_____

_____

_____

_____

❧✦❧

My Personal Notes: _____

_____

_____

_____

_____

_____

_____

_____

_____

_____

_____

_____

_____

_____

_____

_____

_____

_____

_____

_____

_____

_____

❧✦❧

My Personal Notes: _____

_____

_____

_____

_____

_____

_____

_____

_____

_____

_____

_____

_____

_____

_____

_____

_____

_____

_____

_____

_____

_____

_____

❧✦❧

My Personal Notes: _____

_____

_____

_____

_____

_____

_____

_____

_____

_____

_____

_____

_____

_____

_____

_____

_____

_____

_____

_____

_____

_____

_____

_____

_____

❧✦❧

PREDESTINED TO SOAR

You may contact the author, Una Lisa Williams, at
Predestined 2 Soar through the email address below:

Predestined2Soar@gmail.com

About Una Lisa Williams

Una Lisa Williams is a compassionate, energetic, and active community servant leader. She is a mentor, advocate, author, and inspirational speaker who is passionately committed to making a difference in the lives of others, particularly teenagers and young adults. She loves inspiring, encouraging, educating, and empowering others with their personal, spiritual, and professional growth, dreams, goals, and challenges.

Una is proud of her son Matthew, who encourages and supports her frequently. She currently resides in Lawton, Oklahoma and is a native of Donaldsonville, Louisiana.

Una has been employed with the Department of Defense since December 2002. She currently serves as a full-time, nationally certified-recognized professional Sexual Harassment and Assault Victim Advocate, advocating on behalf of individuals of sexual violence. She provides education and training in the areas of prevention, intervention, victim rights, policy, and procedures to military personnel and DOD civilians.

Una is very active in her community and across the state. She is sought out for guidance and advice by individuals of all ages with difficult matters. She dedicates countless hours of her personal time providing resources and tools, conducting training, facilitating open discussions, and advocating on victim rights, civil rights, and healthy relationships throughout and across the state of Oklahoma. She is known and respected for being a knowledgeable, trustworthy, and compassionate leader who is highly inspirational and deeply devoted in her service.

Una is a United States Army Veteran Sergeant, and has served as president since February 2016 (and is one of two original charted members) of the first local Women Veterans chapter, under the umbrella of Oklahoma Women Veterans Organization, HQ.

Una was awarded Oklahoma Women Veteran of the Year in October 2017 and was recognized as "Our Women of The Year" by the Lawton/Fort Sill Chamber of Commerce in March 2018. She was also recognized for her successes by her Brigade Commander, Command Sergeant Major, and the Fort Sill Commanding General, in May 2018. Una has received countless awards over the years for her service and contribution.

Una believes that a heart of passion, giving, and a sincere servant spirit toward others are some of the main ingredients to healthy communities. Additionally, she believes the *Creator of All* has given everyone the gifts and talents unique to their calling and their individual purpose and plan, and that they are already equipped to pursue their missions, dreams, and goals.

Learn more about Una Lisa Williams and her professional achievements and credentials at UnaLisaWilliams.com.

You are Predestined to Soar!

৵♥৸

Splendor Publishing

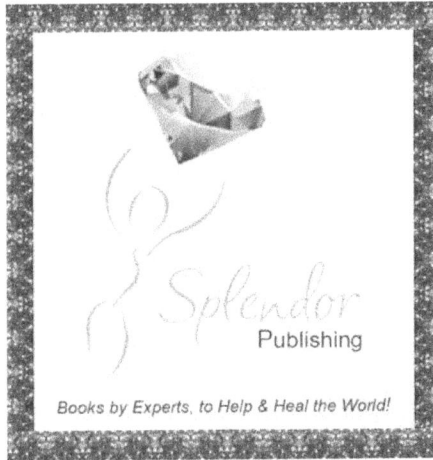

Splendor Publishing's life-changing books are written by skilled and passionate leaders, entrepreneurs, ministers, pastors, and experts who are on a mission to make a positive and significant impact in the lives of others.

Splendor books inspire and encourage personal, professional, and spiritual growth. For information about our book titles, authors, or publishing process, or for wholesale ordering of any of our books for conferences, seminars, events, or training, please visit us at SplendorPublishing.com.

www.ingramcontent.com/pod-product-compliance
Lightning Source LLC
Chambersburg PA
CBHW070019110426
42741CB00034B/2156